D1068463

CHANGING
Families

Multiracial Families

Barbara Sheen

ReferencePoint
Press®

San Diego, CA

About the Author

Barbara Sheen is the author of one hundred books for young people. She lives in New Mexico with her family. In her spare time, she likes to swim, walk, garden, and cook.

For more information, contact:
ReferencePoint Press, Inc.
PO Box 27779
San Diego, CA 92198
www.ReferencePointPress.com

Picture Credits:

Cover: iStock/Thinkstock Images

7: Associated Press
13: Maury Aaseng
16: Rob Hainer/Shutterstock.com
24: FatCamera/iStock.com

27: Page Light Studios/Shutterstock.com
33: FatCamera/iStock.com
40: KGC-03/STAR MAX/IPx/Newscom
44: ABA/Newscom
49: holgs/iStock.com
53: monkeybusinessimages/iStock.com

LIBRARY OF CONGRESS CATALOGING-IN-PUBLICATION DATA

Name: Sheen, Barbara, author.
Title: Multiracial Families/by Barbara Sheen.
Description: San Diego, CA: ReferencePoint Press, [2018] | Series: Changing Families | Audience: Grade 9 to 12. | Includes bibliographical references and index.
Identifiers: LCCN 2018013485 (print) | LCCN 2018014059 (ebook) | ISBN 9781682823620 (eBook) | ISBN 9781682823613 (hardback)
Subjects: LCSH: Interracial marriage—United States—Juvenile literature. | Racially mixed families—United States—Juvenile literature.
Classification: LCC HQ1031 (ebook) | LCC HQ1031 .S464 2018 (print) | DDC 306.84/50973—dc23
LC record available at https://lccn.loc.gov/2018013485

Contents

Chapter One

How American Families Are Changing

Nicole is a teenager whose father is Hispanic and whose mother is African American. Nicole does not have the same skin tone as either of her parents, nor facial features characteristic of a particular ethnic group. In fact, by looking at her, it is difficult to determine Nicole's ethnicity. When people meet Nicole, one of the first things they ask her is, "What are you?" Nicole resents this question because it makes her feel like people are trying to categorize her by her ethnicity instead of getting to know her as a person.

Although Nicole loves who she is, she often struggles with challenges that are unique to multiracial individuals. As she explains, "I'm lucky because I have two cultures. . . . But at the same time, being both has kind of made me self-conscious. People see me in so many different ways. So I'm never sure if people are treating me a certain way because of what I look like or because of who I am. . . . You can't understand it unless you've experienced it."[1]

A Rapidly Growing Group

Some people may find a multiracial/multiethnic family like Nicole's out of sync with what they believe constitutes a typical American family. By definition, a family is a group of people related by blood, marriage, or legal bonds. In the past, a typical American family was made up of a man and woman of the same race and the biological children they shared. However, American families are changing, and mixed-race families, which are also referred to as biracial, interracial, multiracial, or multiethnic families, are rapidly increasing in numbers. Since the 1980s, marriages between

Asians and Caucasians have increased by 1,000 percent, and marriages between African Americans and Caucasians have increased by 400 percent. The 2010 US census, which is the most recent complete census, found that mixed-race couples make up approximately 10 percent of the total US population. This translates to approximately 5.4 million households. Moreover, the number of mixed-race young people is also growing. The US Census Bureau reports an estimated 4.2 million American children and teenagers are mixed race, and their numbers are predicted to triple by 2060. In fact, multiracial kids and teens are the fastest-growing segment of the population. According to Suzy Richardson, the founder of Mixed and Happy, a website that supports multiracial families, "The numbers, for mixed race families like my own, mean that the world must stop and recognize the changing face of today's family, the changing face of today's individual."[2]

Gathering data about mixed-race people and families is a relatively new practice. Statistics concerning these individuals were first collected and tabulated during the 2000 census. Previously, the census required that Americans classify themselves as either a member of a single race or as "other." Starting with the 2000 census, people were given the option to identify as more than one race. Individuals could select any combination of white, black or African American, Native American or Alaskan Native, Asian, Native Hawaiian or other Pacific Islander, or another race. A subheading allowed those who identified as Asian to further clarify their ethnic background by checking off specific Asian nations related to their ancestry. People of any race could also identify as Hispanic, Latino, or Spanish origin, which is the only racialized ethnicity on the form. Under this category, individuals could further describe themselves as Puerto Rican, Cuban, Mexican, another Hispanic or Latino, or

> "The numbers, for mixed race families like my own, mean that the world must stop and recognize the changing face of today's family, the changing face of today's individual."[2]
>
> —Suzy Richardson, the founder of the Mixed and Happy website

Spanish origin. So, mixed-race individuals could check off multiple categories as well as multiple options under each category depending on their background.

Being given the option of declaring their full identity came as a relief to many individuals, who felt like they were being forced to deny a part of themselves in the past. As mixed-race writer and blogger E. Dolores Johnson explains,

> For the first time, the 2000 Census offered an option for mixed race that gave the respondent the chance to self-declare the components of his or her own identity. Dozens of racial and ethnic categories were listed for those who wished to check all the boxes of their multicultural, multi-racial, selves, including a box for white, allowing people like me to acknowledge, legally and honorably, both sides of their heritage. After more than 200 years, the census had stopped dictating who people had to be and asked me to define myself.[3]

A Bitter History

One reason why the US census did not collect and tabulate data about mixed-race Americans before 2000 is that for many years mixed-race relationships were considered socially unacceptable by a large part of American society. And mixed-race people were expected to identify as a minority race. Historically, Caucasians were considered superior to other races in the United States, and interracial relationships were seen as tainting the white race. In fact, until 1967, laws in seventeen states—known as anti-miscegenation laws—banned marriage between whites and nonwhites (primarily blacks but also Native Americans and Asians). Multiracial families often faced prejudice, harassment, and even imprisonment. This changed when Mildred and Richard Loving, a mixed-race (white and black) couple, were sentenced to a year in prison for breaking Virginia's anti-miscegenation law. The Lovings fought the ruling. In 1967 their case went before the US Supreme Court, which found anti-miscegenation laws to be unconstitutional.

In 1958 Richard and Mildred Loving (pictured with their three children) were charged with criminal behavior under Virginia's anti-miscegenation law. Nine years later, they fought the ruling before the US Supreme Court, which struck down the state law as unconstitutional.

The *Loving v. Virginia* case was an important step in changing the ethnic makeup of American families. The civil rights movement of the 1960s, which challenged the idea that one racial group was superior to another, also made racial mixing more acceptable. Indeed, during the early 1960s less than 10 percent of Americans approved of multiracial relationships. In contrast, by the 1990s more than half of all Americans supported these unions, and today individuals who disapprove of multiracial relationships and families are often viewed as racists.

Race Is Not Biological

Many people who opposed interracial relationships were under the misconception that there are large biological differences between the races. In reality, all humans are members of the same species, *Homo sapiens*, and share a common descent. While

Outdated Laws

Even though the Supreme Court declared anti-miscegenation laws unconstitutional in 1967, laws banning mixed-race marriages remained on the books of some states for many years. Although not enforceable, these laws were supported by some Americans.

As an article on Loving Day, a website that supports annual celebrations to honor the Supreme Court's ruling, explains,

> Incredibly, laws against interracial couples stayed on the books for decades after the Loving decision. In 1998, a clause that prohibited "marriage of a white person with a Negro . . . or a person who shall have one-eighth or more Negro blood" was removed from South Carolina's state constitution. According to a Mason-Dixon poll four months before the vote, 22% of South Carolina voters were opposed to the removal of this clause. . . . In Alabama, it took until 2000 to remove these laws. . . . According to a poll conducted by the Mobile [Alabama] Register in September of 2000, 19% of voters said that they would not remove [this law]. Because of the Loving decision, these laws were not legally enforceable after June 12th, 1967—even though they were on the books.

Loving Day, "The Last Laws to Go: 1998 and 2000." www.lovingday.org.

there is genetic diversity between all people, no matter their race, biological differences between the races are minuscule. Any two unrelated white people, for example, are as genetically different from each other as they are from two people of any other race. And although there are physical differences between people living in different regions, these differences are due to hereditary factors as well as social and environmental ones. For example, skin color or hair texture can be explained as an adaptation to climate and environment, and body size and shape can be related to lifestyle and nutritional factors. According to sociologists George Yancey and Richard Lewis Jr.,

Biological differences have relatively little to do with how we define distinct racial groups. Not all Blacks have darker skin than all Whites. Not all Asians are shorter than all Hispanics. These . . . differences, on their own, cannot be used to determine the racial category to which people belong. Thus, racial membership is heavily determined by the definitions provided in the particular society.[4]

Indeed, race is actually a social construct that is used to categorize people. It has also been used as a way for one group to establish superior social status over another and use this status for personal gain. For instance, the belief that white people were biologically superior to blacks or Native Americans was a way for white people to justify slavery or the taking of Native American tribal lands.

This ideology resulted in unequal treatment of nonwhites, including multiracial individuals. Although this kind of thinking is not common today, it has not completely disappeared. Therefore, multiracial people with darker skin tones still often face prejudice. A mixed-race man of Asian and black heritage comments, "Maybe I'm wrong, but it depends on what two races you are. If you're Asian and Hispanic and you come out with fair skin . . . I think you're always going to be perceived as better than [those who are] brown or darker, or darker skinned."[5]

> "Biological differences have relatively little to do with how we define distinct racial groups. Not all Blacks have darker skin than all Whites. Not all Asians are shorter than all Hispanics. These . . . differences, on their own, cannot be used to determine the racial category to which people belong."[4]
>
> —Sociologists George Yancey and Richard Lewis Jr.

How Multiracial Families Form

With changes in the law and growing public acceptance of racial mixing, more and more people are entering into relationships with partners of a different ethnicity or race. These individuals often fall in love and have a family, which is one of the ways multiracial families come to be. Some multiracial families form when partners bring mixed-race children from a former relationship into the household. Adoptive families, too, are often multiracial. This is known as transracial adoption. In the United States, most prospective adoptive parents are white. But most children who are available for adoption are of other races or ethnicities. Therefore, it is not unusual for these adoptions to involve, but not be limited to, a white heterosexual or same-sex couple and a minority or mixed-race child. Some transracial adoptive families form when prospective parents adopt an orphan from another country.

Both national and international transracial adoptions have become more common during the last fifty years. The 2010 census found that 40 percent of all adoptions are transracial. In the past, these adoptions were controversial. Out of fear that kids raised in a different culture would grow up ignorant of their cultural heritage, many people believed that adopted children did best in families of the same race. Most adoption agencies supported this concept. As a result, prospective parents and children were matched on the basis of their ethnicity. This practice left many prospective parents without children, and vice versa. However, as acceptance of multiracial families has evolved, so, too, has acceptance of transracial adoptions. Moreover, to ensure that young people are knowledgeable about their ethnic heritage, many adoptive parents make a point of educating their children about their native culture.

What Do Multiracial Families Look Like?

Multiracial families have many faces. Unlike in single-race families, family members in multiracial families may not bear a close resemblance to each other. Skin tone, hair texture and color, eye color, and physical features can vary significantly among family members. Couples of different races usually look very different from each other. Their children may resemble one parent more than the other, have some resemblance to both, or look com-

Celebrities and Transracial Adoptions

Many celebrities choose to raise multiracial families. Some of these individuals have adopted children from poor or war-torn countries, where there are many more orphans than prospective parents. If they are not adopted, most of these children wind up living in orphanages or even on the street. The family of actors Brad Pitt and Angelina Jolie is among the most well-known. The divorced couple shares six children. They have three biological children, and they have three adopted children from Cambodia, Ethiopia, and Vietnam.

Other celebrities, like actor Hugh Jackman and his wife, adopted multiracial children born in the United States. The couple has two children: a son of Native American, African American, Caucasian, and Hawaiian heritage and a daughter of Mexican and German heritage. From the start, the couple wanted to adopt children who were most in need. Says Jackman,

> When we went first to talk to someone in Los Angeles about adoption, I remember, they said, "What do you want?" I said, "Well, healthy would be good. And they said, "Well, what about the race?" We'd ticked [selected] mixed race. And he said, "Now, listen. Please don't, please don't just tick that because you think it's the right thing to tick." And he said to me, that we turn away children every month who are mixed race, because we can't find families for them.

Hearing this, the Jackmans insisted on adopting mixed-race children.

Quoted in Daniel S. Levine, "Oscar & Ava, Hugh Jackman's Kids: 5 Fast Facts You Need to Know," Heavy, March 2, 2017. https://heavy.com.

pletely different from either one. As Kathleen Ojo, a white female blogger married to an African man, writes,

> Every parent wonders who their baby will take after, how their features will blend to create a unique, yet similar, little person. Being from such different ethnic backgrounds, and looking as different from each other as we do, the

spectrum was vast—Amaliya [the couple's daughter] could have come out with very dark skin, very light skin, or anything in between. Her facial features, as she grows, may gravitate more towards Caucasian or African, or both, or neither.[6]

Siblings, too, may look alike or look very different from each other depending on the genes they inherit. For instance, whereas a boy with an Asian father and a black mother might have almond-shaped eyes, pale skin, and curly dark hair, his sister may have brown skin, straight hair, and round eyes. In her book *Born Beautiful Biracial*, writer Tanya Hutchins compiled a series of essays written by multiracial children. A six-year-old named Queen Afradeshia, is one of these children. She wrote: "My brother Zac is white, my sister Titi is kinda like me and my sister Ruthie is a little like me."[7]

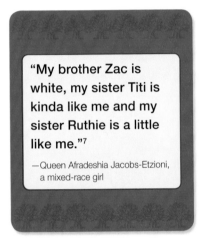

"My brother Zac is white, my sister Titi is kinda like me and my sister Ruthie is a little like me."[7]

—Queen Afradeshia Jacobs-Etzioni, a mixed-race girl

Who Intermarries?

Although multiracial families are composed of people with a range of ethnic and racial backgrounds, some ethnic and racial groups are more likely to intermarry than others. A 2015 Pew Research Center report found that of all marriages in the United States 58 percent of Native Americans, 28 percent of Asians, 19 percent of blacks, and 7 percent of whites married someone of a different race. It also reports that nearly one-quarter of all Hispanics marry someone of a different ethnicity.

The same survey found that there are gender differences in who intermarries within some racial groups. Black men, for example, are more likely to intermarry than black women. The opposite is true for Asians and Native Americans. In these groups, women are more likely to marry someone of a different race than are Asian or Native American men.

A Growing Population

Since 1980, the percentage of multiracial/multiethnic babies born in the United States has almost tripled. Multiracial or multiethnic children are defined as those whose parents are two different races or ethnicities—for example, children with one Hispanic and one non-Hispanic parent, or those with at least one parent who identifies as multiracial. The graph illustrates the increase in multiracial/multiethnic children under the age of one, living with two parents. Of the 14 percent who fit that description in 2015, the most common combination is children with one Hispanic and one white parent.

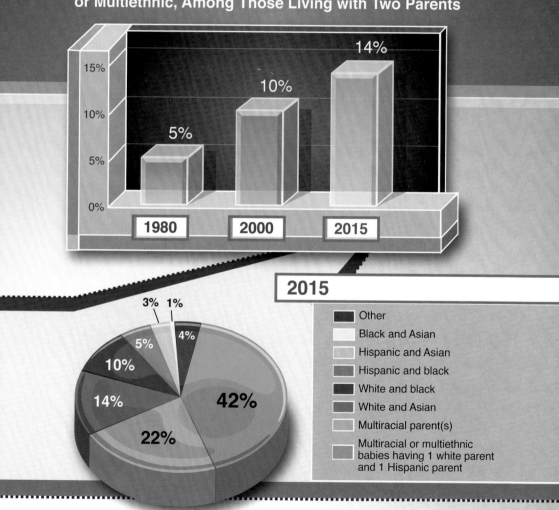

% of Children Younger than One Who Are Multiracial or Multiethnic, Among Those Living with Two Parents

1980: 5%
2000: 10%
2015: 14%

2015

- Other
- Black and Asian
- Hispanic and Asian
- Hispanic and black
- White and black
- White and Asian
- Multiracial parent(s)
- Multiracial or multiethnic babies having 1 white parent and 1 Hispanic parent

Pie chart values: 42%, 22%, 14%, 10%, 5%, 4%, 3%, 1%

Note: Whites, blacks, and Asians include only non-Hispanics. Hispanics are of any race. Asians include Pacific Islanders; pie chart total does not equal 100 percent due to rounding.

Source: Kristen Bialik, "Key Facts About Race and Marriage, 50 Years After *Loving v. Virginia*," Pew Research Center, June 12, 2017. www.pewresearch.org.

Where and How Do Multiracial Families Live?

Multiracial families live all over the United States. Certain regions have a larger multiracial population than others. And some racial pairings are more common in some regions than they are in others. For example, the largest number of couples consisting of a Hispanic and another race reside in the Southwest, and, according to *Business Insider* magazine, the largest number of black/white couples is found in Virginia, Maryland, and Washington, DC.

With 23.6 percent of the population identifying as multiracial, Hawaii has the greatest number of multiracial individuals and families. Most are a mixture of white and either Asian or Pacific Islander. But other ethnic mixtures are found here too. Other states and regions with large multiracial populations include Alaska, Oklahoma, the West Coast, the Southwest, and the mid-Atlantic region.

Mixed-race couples in these states and regions, as well as in other parts of the country, are having children. According to a Pew Research Center report, in 2015, 44 percent of all infants born in Hawaii were multiracial or multiethnic, as were 28 percent born in Alaska and Oklahoma, 22 percent in California and Nevada, and 18 percent in Washington and Oregon. But no matter where multiracial families live or their cultural mix, most live no differently than other types of families. Rachelle Chapman is an African American woman who is married to a white man; their child is biracial. She says, "What brings us together is far more important than what separates us."[8]

Chapter Two

How I See Myself and My Family

A variety of factors impact the way young people perceive themselves and their families. These factors include their age and physical appearance, how and where they are raised, and the racial or ethnic makeup of other family members.

A Changing View

Multiracial youth frequently see themselves and their families in differing ways at various stages in their lives. For instance, young children are aware of differences in people's skin color and appearance, but they do not distinguish between racial groups. Even if members of their family look very different from each other, young children accept this as normal. As Allison Bates, a mixed-race young woman, remembers, "In the neighborhoods where I lived, I could see white people and black people and brown people and yellow people, but I never placed my parents in these categories. I never saw my parents' race, and so my mother wasn't my 'white' mom and my father wasn't my 'black' dad until I was probably thirteen."[9]

Likewise, young children do not view themselves as different from other people. Brian, a young man whose mother is Asian and whose father is white, recalls, "When I was really young, I thought I was like everyone else. I had almost no ethnic identity. It was not defined yet, whereas now it is. So it must have developed somewhere along the way."[10]

Over time, and with more exposure to society, children begin to notice racial differences within their family as well as between themselves and others. For example, author Debra Dickerson is African American. She and her Caucasian husband have two children. The family lives in a white neighborhood and, with the exception of Dickerson, the children rarely see people of color. She explains how her light-skinned, blond six-year-old son became more aware of racial differences in the family:

> I took him to an inner-city event and everybody was black, basically . . . and he was so confused. He kept looking around. . . . And he's going Mommy, why is everybody brown? Why is everybody brown? It's, like, well Mommy's brown and, you know, that just did not compute. And then, a couple days later, he asked me if I'd been burned at some point. And I said, what do you mean? He thought that would explain why I was brown all over. . . . It's only just now starting to dawn on him these racial differences.[11]

Some children of multiracial families struggle with how their appearance differs noticeably from their parents or even their siblings. Others simply accept their inherited features and choose to see themselves as a beautiful blending of two or more cultural heritages.

As kids mature, their own appearance and the appearance of their family often become an issue, affecting how they see themselves. If they look significantly different from the rest of their family, some kids and teens see themselves as weird or unattractive. They may do things like relaxing or coloring their hair, wearing colored contact lenses, or spending time in the sun to darken their skin in an effort to look more like other family members.

Other multiracial young people celebrate their differences. Rather than letting their appearance separate them from the rest of their family, they see themselves as a beautiful blend of two or more cultures. Nine-year-old Ailish falls into this group. "Being biracial is a gift," she says.

> "If someone was having a hard time I would tell them that 'you are special, beautiful and biracial. Not many people are biracial, that you have a gift, and not too many people have that gift.'"[12]
>
> —Ailish Elzy, a mixed-race girl

> My dad is black and my mom is white and I came out just right. . . . Being a different color makes me feel special. I am not too white and I am not too black and that makes me different. . . . If someone was having a hard time I would tell them that "you are special, beautiful and biracial. Not many people are biracial, that you have a gift, and not too many people have that gift."[12]

How Where They Live Affects Young People

Where multiracial young people live also affects how they perceive themselves and their family. Those who live in communities where there is a diverse population usually feel more comfortable and accepting of themselves and their families than those who live in less ethnically diverse communities. Growing up in an ethnically diverse community exposes kids to other families similar to their own. This makes youngsters feel like they and their family fit in. Moreover, in ethnically diverse communities multiracial families and individuals

Some Multiracial Kids Feel Privileged

Some multiracial kids and teens see themselves as privileged. Many of these young people grow up in solidly middle-class families, where they are given many advantages that poorer youngsters do not have. According to a Pew Research Center report, most multiracial/multiethnic families are financially comfortable. The median annual income for mixed-race couples is higher than that for same-race couples. For example, the median annual income of Asian/white couples is approximately $71,000. It is $57,900 for Hispanic/white couples and $53,187 for black/white couples. In contrast, it is $62,000 for Asian couples; $60,000 for white couples; $36,000 for Hispanic couples, and $47,700 for black couples.

Multiracial couples are also more likely to have a higher level of education than individuals who marry within their own race. For instance, almost half of all white individuals married to Asians have college degrees, compared to an estimated one-third of whites married to other whites. As Sierra, a mixed-race teen of Asian and white heritage, explains, "I enjoy a lot of privileges. I'm middle class and I go to a good school."

Sierra Fang-Horvath, "Mixed Race Privilege?," KQED Radio, March 9, 2017. ww2.kqed.org.

are less likely to be discriminated against or treated differently. Journalist Nadra Kareem Nittle writes,

> The more diverse a city is, the higher the chances that a number of interracial couples and multiethnic children live there. Although living in such an area won't guarantee that your children never face problems because of their heritage, it lessens the odds that your child will be viewed as an anomaly and your family subjected to rude stares and other bad behavior when out and about.[13]

In school, students growing up in ethnically mixed communities usually have racially diverse classmates. As a result, multiracial kids are more likely to be accepted by their peers and to see themselves as normal rather than as an oddity. Chris Collado, a young man of Afro-Cuban and white heritage, comments,

> At different points in my childhood, my family lived in New Jersey and Southern California. Both of these communities had diverse populations. . . . I had classmates who were of different racial backgrounds and ethnicities; the fact that there were many children of color made racial diversity the norm. I was aware of the fact that I had darker-colored skin, curly hair, and dark brown eyes, but I didn't think much of it because everyone was a little different.[14]

In contrast, young people who grow up in less diverse regions are more likely to stand out. People may openly stare at them and their families, make insensitive remarks, and ask rude or prying questions about their background. Kids may be teased at school because they look different. Although these young people may see themselves and their family as normal in the privacy of their homes, they often feel conspicuous, embarrassed, or uncomfortable when they are out in public. As a result, their self-esteem may suffer, and they may try to blend into the dominant culture of the region, even if it means denying all or part of their own heritage.

Cultural Influences

Cultural factors also influence the way young people view themselves and their families. Multiracial families are a mixture of at least two cultures. In some families, both cultures are celebrated. In these families, kids are exposed to diverse foods, holidays, traditions, and celebrations. Likewise, they are given ample opportunities to spend time with family members from all sides of the family. This helps young people understand and feel part of the cultures that formed them. As a result, these kids are likely to embrace the different components of their ethnic heritage and feel comfortable with who they are, which helps boost their self-worth. Moreover, because they are around multiple cultures as they mature, these young people often see themselves as open-minded and tolerant of other people, no matter their ethnicity. Fariba Soetan, a multiracial blogger currently raising three mixed-race children with her Nigerian husband, writes,

> We want our children to not only know their extended families but also to know where they are from, where their parents grew up, their family histories. The fact that our families live on different continents makes for some amazing holidays and a cultural experience that we may not have anywhere else—the food, the celebrations. . . . With multiple excuses to celebrate and feast . . . we get twice the number of festivals and celebrations as anyone else! For my family, we go from Nowruz (Persian New Year) to Easter in one week! If you're Chinese, you get to celebrate Valentine's Day and Chinese New Year so close together you might as well permanently eat chocolate! With so many festivals and celebrations bringing together family, friends, food and often music, your kids will get to experience the richness and diversity of multiple cultures. And that's never a bad thing.[15]

Some families, on the other hand, emphasize only one culture. Children in these families often feel distant from the neglected part of their heritage and from people of that ethnic background. They may feel confused about their own identity or may be resentful because that part of their culture is ignored. "I don't feel a connection to Filipinos," says Miriam, a multiracial teenager whose family largely ignored her Filipino heritage while she was growing up. "If I was in a crowded room and I was looking for a connection with someone, I wouldn't go up to an Asian person, because I've never been around the culture. I don't know anything about it. I don't speak the language. . . . I know that that's what I am, but I don't identify with it like, 'Those are my people.'"[16]

Whether or not race and racial issues are discussed at home also influences the way young people see themselves and their families. Talking about issues such as racial discrimination helps kids to understand the challenges they may face from some members of society and provides them with survival skills to deal with these challenges. It also makes them aware that unfair treatment, if it occurs, might have nothing to do with anything they have said or done; rather, it is due to racism. Without this awareness, kids and teens are more likely to take unfair treatment personally. This can affect their psychological well-being and lessen their self-confidence. As author Sarah H. Chang stresses, "It is beyond incredibly important to talk to multiracial . . . kids about race . . . because they are . . . [multiracial] people in a racist society."[17]

> "It is beyond incredibly important to talk to multiracial . . . kids about race . . . because they are [multiracial] people in a racist society."[17]
>
> —Sarah H. Chang, author

Feeling Isolated

Many multiracial kids and teens embrace the various cultures that are their heritage and are proud of who they are. However, those who do not have a lot of contact with other young people who share their specific ethnic background sometimes feel like they have no one with whom they can share their unique experiences and feelings. This makes them feel isolated. "For some of us in the mixed race community, our mix feels very singular, rare. Perhaps something like being a unicorn in a field of horses,"[18] says Jennifer, a young woman of Sri Lankan and black heritage.

Many multiracial young people also feel that their differences separate them from single-race people, even when they share a part of those people's ethnicity. In order to fit in and be accepted, mixed-race individuals often present themselves in ways that emphasize one particular part of their culture while excluding the rest of their heritage. They do this by adopting the mannerisms, language, and clothing associated with a specific ethnic group. For instance, individuals of Hispanic and black heritage might speak Spanish, eat certain foods, and listen to certain kinds of music in order to be accepted by other Hispanics. But in situations in which they are around blacks, they might present themselves in ways associated with African American culture. As Thomas, a mixed-race young man, explains, "I can be white. I can be Asian, or I can be somewhere in between, depending on what suits me at the time."[19]

This chameleon-like behavior allows many multiracial people to move between different cultures. However, it also causes some of these youngsters to feel like posers. They believe that their acceptance by each group is based on who they appear to be rather than who they really are. And, if they were to expose their complete selves, some fear they would be rejected by both groups. Consequently, they see themselves as caught between two worlds, and not really fitting into either. According to Andrew Garrod, Robert Kilkenny, and Christina Gomez, the editors of the book *Mixed*, "They understand that they inhabit a separate space that is often 'in between.'"[20]

> "My whole identity isn't acknowledged [and] I'm assumed to be an outsider in almost every space I enter. That is a very isolating feeling."[21]
>
> —Ariana Brown, multiethnic poet

According to the Pew Research Center, approximately one out of every eight multiracial adults says they have felt like an outsider at some time in their lives because of their mixed-racial background. Award-winning multiethnic poet Ariana Brown says, "My whole identity isn't acknowledged [and] I'm assumed to be an outsider in almost every space I enter. That is a very isolating feeling."[21]

Home Sweet Home

Although multiracial young people may sometimes feel isolated or different outside their homes, when they are at home with their families, most feel secure and loved. Kidada Jones grew up feel-

Important Terms

A number of different terms are used by social scientists when discussing race and multiracial people and families. Some of these terms are interchangeable, and young people may use a variety of these terms in describing themselves. The list below defines some of the most commonly used terms:

African American: An American whose ancestors came from Africa. This term may be used interchangeably with *black* to denote race.

Afro-Asian: A person of African and Asian descent.

Asian American: An American whose ancestors came from Asia.

bicultural: A person whose heritage is composed of two cultures.

biracial: A person whose biological parents are two different races.

Caucasian: A person with light skin, usually of European descent. This term is used interchangeably with *white* to denote race.

Hapa: A Hawaiian term for a person who is part Asian or part Pacific Islander.

Hispanic: A person of Spanish-speaking ancestry. This term is used interchangeably with *Latino, Latina,* and *Latinx.*

hybrid: A person whose biological parents are two different races.

multiracial: A person whose racial heritage is composed of two or more races. This term is used interchangeably with *mixed race, multiethnic,* and *biracial.*

multiracial family: A family in which the members are made up of two or more races. This term is used interchangeably with *mixed-race, interracial,* or *multiethnic family.*

Native American: A person of American Indian ancestry. This term is used interchangeably with *Amerindian.*

ing this way. The mixed-race daughter of musician Quincy Jones and actress Peggy Lipton recalls, "We had a sweet, encapsulated family. We were our own little world. . . . There's the warmth of love inside a family, and then there's the outside world."[22]

Not only do they feel secure at home, many multiracial children have a great deal of respect for their parents. They see their

Children of mixed-race families often learn lessons of tolerance and acceptance from their parents. They commonly exhibit these attitudes in their own interpersonal relationships, looking beyond race or ethnicity and focusing on more important qualities in others.

parents as trailblazers who got together despite societal disapproval. In many cases, their parents faced harassment, discrimination, and a lack of acceptance by friends and family members. And they frequently dealt with unpleasant comments and prying questions from neighbors, work associates, and even strangers. Most kids view their parents with a great deal of admiration for facing these obstacles in order to be together. Kidada's sister, actress Rashida Jones, agrees: "My mother shocked her Jewish parents by marrying out of her religion and race. And my father: growing up poor and black, bucking the odds and becoming so successful, having the attitude of 'I love this woman!' We're going to have babies and to hell with anyone who doesn't like it! . . . I wouldn't trade my family for anything."[23]

It is not uncommon for these young people to be inspired by the strength of their parent's love and to look beyond race when forming their own relationships. Mixed-race actor Shemar Moore, for example, says that his parents' relationship has inspired him to ignore race in his own relationships. "I think love is blind. I'm half black, half white."[24] Clearly, multiracial individuals view themselves and their families in many ways. Despite facing challenges unique to growing up in a multiracial family, most are proud of who they are and embrace the special bond they share with their families.

Chapter Three

How Others See Me and My Family

Multiracial individuals and families are viewed by others in a variety of ways. How others see them impacts the lives of young people both positively and negatively. According to Chester, a young man of Chinese, Japanese, and European American heritage, "I am always worried about how people are going to look at me. Are they going to accept me for . . . who I am? It's not a problem within myself—it's a problem with how people look at me."[25]

Indeed, in an effort to avoid frustrating situations or pressure from others, multiracial individuals sometimes have to reconcile the way other people see them with the way they see themselves. At other times, they must disregard the way others see them in order to remain true to the way they see themselves. As a young man named Brandon comments,

> My mother is Filipino with a little bit of Chinese, and my father is a whole hodgepodge of Western European things. And I grew up in a predominantly white community in Maine. And in a way I consider myself privileged to have had that upbringing just because being all of these things really gave me a perspective on how fluid race and ethnicity are and how socially constructed they are. I think it's very important to differentiate between how others see you and how you see yourself or how I see myself.[26]

An Object of Curiosity

In most families, family members resemble each other. Multiracial family members, however, are out of the ordinary. Not all family members share the same ethnicity, and they frequently look significantly different from each other. Society tends to categorize people by race or ethnicity. Multiracial families are difficult to categorize, which makes them the object of intense curiosity. It is not uncommon for multiracial families to be stared at and treated differently than single-race families. And their familial relationship is often questioned. Twelve-year-old Rebecca comments, "I am African-American, Hispanic, and Caucasian. . . . Sometimes when my family has gone someplace where most people are one race, people have looked at us funny (both of my parents are white because I am adopted). It used to bother me when people looked at me that way."[27]

It is not unusual for people who do not know the family to assume that a parent and child who look racially different from each other are unrelated. There are many incidences in which parents have been mistaken for a nanny, babysitter, or even a kidnapper. When others cannot see the connection and love between these family members, it makes kids and parents feel like the validity of their family is being questioned. This can make both parents and kids feel uncomfortable and hurt. Ealoni Friedenthal, a mixed-race young woman, describes some of her experiences:

> I grew up the second daughter of a Black mother and Jewish father. . . . I have very pale skin and freckles with red hair. . . . All my childhood and even to this day, when I go places with my mom, people assume she's my nanny or friend. . . . When I was a toddler, a woman in the grocery store accused my mother of kidnapping me because I was

> "I am African-American, Hispanic, and Caucasian. . . . Sometimes when my family has gone someplace where most people are one race, people have looked at us funny (both of my parents are white because I am adopted). It used to bother me when people looked at me that way."[27]
>
> —Rebecca Brestel, a multiracial girl

throwing a temper tantrum in the cereal aisle and [she] went and got the store manager. People make assumptions based on the color of one's skin without taking into account how the others involved might react.[28]

Family members often face comments from strangers and acquaintances who think it is acceptable to pry into the family's background and then make judgmental statements based on their own biases. Upon learning their background, some individuals praise the family for breaking racial barriers, but others make hurtful comments. For instance, when journalist Nevin Martell, who is a white man married to an African woman, was

Because society tends to categorize people by color or ethnicity, children and parents in mixed-race families often attract the curiosity of onlookers. Sometimes outsiders assume that people in multiracial families are not related or they feel entitled to question that relationship.

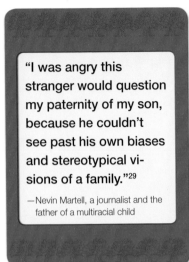

in a café with his three-year-old son, a stranger confronted Martell, questioning the pair's relationship. When Martell explained that they were father and son, the stranger became irritated and accused Martell of lying. "It wasn't until I was sitting in the car that I realized how upset I was," Martell explains. "I was angry this stranger would question my paternity of my son, because he couldn't see past his own biases and stereotypical visions of a family. . . . And I was outraged that anyone would think they had a right to confront a parent in such a way. Unfortunately, my experience is in no way unique."[29]

Parents of multiracial children commonly deal with insensitive comments from people they hardly know. Korean American writer and editor Nicole S. Chung, whose husband is white, recounts some of her experiences:

> People . . . have asked if I am my daughters' baby sitter, presumably because they cannot spot the resemblance between us. At a party last year, a white woman asked if I was surprised when my children were born: "Did you expect them to look, you know, less white?". . . There was the mother at the park who looked at my girls on the swing set and said bluntly: "What are they, exactly?". . . It never fails to throw me when anyone demands to know my daughters' precise ethnic makeup . . . or asks whether such white-looking children really do belong to me.[30]

What Are You?

The same curiosity that makes people confront adult members of mixed-race families also affects kids. Because of their ambigu-

An Exotic Appearance

Because of their unique appearance, multiethnic individuals are often described as exotic looking. Although the term *exotic* is not meant to be derogatory, many multiethnic individuals do not like this label. Since the word *exotic* is a synonym for *strange* or *alien*, they feel that describing mixed-race people as exotic looking is a way to emphasize that they do not fit in and further separate them from the majority of people. According to multiethnic blogger Anjali Patel, "When people call me 'exotic' as if it's a compliment, it's not—it's a blatant act of othering [making one feel different]. It instantly comes across as a thinly veiled way of saying, 'You look different, but in an aesthetically acceptable way.'"

Moreover, since the exotic label is used to describe all multiethnic people, it makes some mixed-race young people feel like they are being stereotyped rather than being seen as unique individuals. As Patel explains, "To say anything that generalizes literally millions of people is . . . never going to be anything but offensive and dehumanizing."

Anjali Patel, "18 Things Mixed Race Girls Are Very Tired of People Saying to Them," Bustle, March 18, 2015. www .bustle.com.

ous appearance, multiracial young people are often questioned about their ethnicity. Most report being asked, "What are you?" multiple times in their lives. It is often the first thing people say upon meeting them. Some kids and teens like it when others ask them this question because it gives them a chance to show their pride in their multicultural heritage. Others, however, do not. Being questioned about their ethnicity makes some kids feel like they are some sort of oddity. Some young people even find the phrasing of the question disrespectful. "What people mean to ask me is, 'What is your race?,' 'What is your cultural heritage?,' 'What's your ethnicity?' However, it's rarely phrased like that,"[31] says Alanna, a multiethnic blogger.

Multiracial Families Throughout the World

Multiracial families are found all over the world. In fact, mixed-race people make up the majority of the population in Latin America and the Caribbean. There are also large numbers of multiethnic people and families in Europe—especially in the United Kingdom, France, Italy, Spain, and the Netherlands—as well as in Canada, Australia, New Zealand, and parts of Asia. Indeed, 11.2 percent of New Zealanders identify as mixed race. Of these individuals, about 23 percent are under the age of fifteen.

Many mixed-race families throughout the world can trace their roots back to the early history of their country. Colonization brought white Europeans and African slaves to Latin America and the Caribbean. Intermarriage between the indigenous people, white Europeans, and black Africans was quite common. In many Latin American and Caribbean nations, being multiracial is the norm. In fact, in Brazil 38.5 percent of the population is multiracial. Similarly, intermarriage between French fur traders and the aboriginal people of Canada was widespread. Likewise, colonization, wars, and trade brought people from other nations to Asia, where multiracial families that are a mix of European and Asian are common.

Today mixed-race individuals and families are a part of many nations. Depending on the nation and its history, in many places these individuals and families are seen and treated no differently than single-race people.

Moreover, many people feel that being questioned about their ethnicity, (often before the questioner even asks their name) is a way to categorize them without getting to know them personally. Nineteen-year-old Jordan explains, "People constantly ask me my ethnicity—I'm Black/Chinese/Norwegian but that doesn't DEFINE who I am. . . . I don't want to be CATEGORIZED. . . . I'm just a HUMAN BEING."[32]

Also, many young people feel that their ethnic background is personal; being asked "What are you?" by people they hardly know is rude and intrusive. Still, most attempt to answer. However, when kids and teens explain their background, they get a mix of responses. Some people admire their diversity while others have trouble accepting it. These individuals are more comfortable classifying multiracial young people as members of one race, usually based on their skin color, their ability to speak a second language, or other physical or cultural traits—even if this is not the way multiracial kids and teens see themselves. In fact, it is not unusual for some people to contradict multiethnic people if they are not happy with their response, which can be both exasperating and hurtful. Amber, a mixed-race teen, says, "No one gets to decide what 'race' they're born as, but a lot of people have the privilege of being able to say 'I'm black,' or 'I'm white,' or 'I'm native American,' etc, without anyone questioning or refuting the statement, based on what they think you're allowed to call yourself."[33]

Chris, a young man whose mother is white and whose father is Afro-Cuban, agrees: "It can be so frustrating to have the very part of you that makes you unique ignored. For the longest time, I couldn't understand why people saw me as anything but . . . mixed."[34] To satisfy these people and avoid awkward situations, some young people tailor their response to whatever they think the questioner wants to hear. Therefore, if they have dark skin, they may respond that they are African American, and if they speak Spanish, they may answer that they are Hispanic despite the fact that this is not how they see themselves.

Extended Family

Just as nonfamily members view multiracial kids in many ways, so, too, do extended family members. In many cases, grandparents, aunts, uncles, and cousins view and treat multiracial family members the same as they do other family members. However, there are exceptions. Bigotry can cause some extended family members to view multiracial relatives as inferior. They may show favoritism toward family members who share their race, which is hurtful and can make youngsters feel rejected by their loved ones.

Due to prejudice and societal pressure, some relatives cut off all contact with the mixed-race family. This usually occurs when an interracial couple marries or when a single-race couple adopts children of a different race. As a result, some mixed-race kids grow up feeling alienated from one side of their family and that part of their ethnic heritage. Mel and Gloria, for example, are single-race parents of two adopted multiracial daughters. Mel's father refuses to have anything to do with the family and has never met his granddaughters. Gloria's mother, on the other hand, adores the children. Gloria's father is not as enthusiastic. "My mom really loves them. She takes them everywhere," Gloria explains. "My dad surprised me because, although he loves them a lot, he still doesn't treat them as good as the other grandkids. But Mama sews them clothes and bakes cookies for them. . . . The kids love her a lot too."[35]

Even when extended family members love and support multiracial families, it is not unusual for someone to inadvertently make an ethnically insensitive remark in front of their multiracial relatives. Single-race black family members, for example, might say something insensitive about white people in the presence of a multiethnic relative who is part white. If the multiethnic relative points out that this type of remark is offensive, he or she is likely to be criticized for being overly sensitive. And the person who made the insensitive comment may go on to explain that the comment does not apply to their relatives but rather to other people. Nevertheless, such comments are hurtful and can cause kids to feel like they are not truly accepted by their loved ones.

Dealing with Peers

Multiracial kids and teens also cope with challenges from their peers. Although many mixed-race individuals are well accepted

Because mixed-race teens and kids might look different than their peers in either of their blended backgrounds, they sometimes feel isolated. They may be teased or bullied because they do not fit clearly into one racial category or another.

by their peers, in some cases, they are not. Children and adolescents are often uncomfortable with anyone who is out of the ordinary and can be cruel to anyone who looks different. As a result, some mixed-race young people are made fun of, bullied, or ostracized simply because of their ethnicity. While growing up, Bridget, a young woman of African American and white heritage, says, "I've been called zebra, Oreo, mud, dirty."[36]

Moreover, this type of treatment can come from all quarters. A teen of Native American and white heritage, for example, may be mistreated by peers belonging to both groups. In many American schools and universities same-race individuals tend to hang out with each other. In order to fit in, some young people will try to align themselves with one particular racial group. Sometimes they are welcomed into the group, but in other cases they are not fully accepted. Group members often see them as not truly Asian or Native American, for example. As a result, they do not believe they share cultural connections or are able to understand the challenges that members of that particular group face. Donna Maketa Randolph, a young woman of Korean American and African American heritage, says, "If you look at me, I'm dark. . . . But I'm not black. For most of the black people at Cornell [University], I am a little too light. But with the Asian people, I'm too dark. So I don't get acknowledged on either side."[37]

Dating

The way others view multiracial young people sometimes impacts whom they date—and the ethnicity of the individuals they date can also influence how others see them. In the eyes of their peers, the ethnicity of the people whom multiracial teens choose to date serves as a way to affirm which cultural group they identify with. According to Monina, whose father is Puerto Rican and mother is African American,

> If I date a black guy, from the black community I get, "She's being true, she knows who she is." And if I date a Hispanic guy, it's like, "She's leaning more that way." If I date an Asian guy it's like, "What's wrong with her? She just wants to forsake everyone." Whatever partner I choose says something. . . . I can't make any choice without thinking at some level, even if only subconsciously, "What are people going to think?" "What are people going to say?"[38]

Consequently, some young people choose to date individuals associated with the group they want to fit into.

Sometimes multiethnic teens are limited in whom they date due to racism or social pressure. Some narrow-minded individuals do not want to date someone who is mixed race, and others fear that their friends might criticize them for doing so. In other cases, family members of single-race kids may prevent some teens from having a relationship with someone who is multiethnic. Historically, darker-skinned people have been seen as inferior to lighter-skinned ones in the United States. This bias seems to be especially strong toward multiracial teens who are part African American. Ashlee Manuel, a mixed-race teen who is part black, fits into this group. As she explains,

> "Most of my friends are white, and their parents won't let them go out with or date biracial kids. That really makes me mad because it doesn't matter the person's outside color or looks! It's inside that counts!"[39]
>
> —Ashlee Manuel, a multiracial teenager

Most of my friends are white, and their parents won't let them go out with or date biracial kids. That really makes me mad because it doesn't matter the person's outside color or looks! It's inside that counts! So, when one of my friends likes a person of a different color, they have to break up with them or they get in trouble. I ask my friends why it matters and they told me that their parents told them it's because blacks and white don't go together.[39]

Clearly, being a multiethnic person is complicated. These young people cannot easily be categorized. How others see them and their families is often influenced by prejudice and social pressure. However, these kids and teens are no different from other people and want to be accepted by others for the unique individuals they are.

Chapter Four

Other People Who Have Families Like Mine

Many well-known, successful people are members of multiracial families. These individuals include Barack Obama, Meghan Markle, and Bruno Mars, among others. They faced challenges related to being multiracial, embraced who they are, and achieved great things.

The Forty-Fourth President of the United States

Former president Barack Obama is one of the most famous multiethnic individuals in history. He was born in Honolulu, Hawaii, on August 4, 1961, to a white mother, Stanley Ann Dunham (called Ann), and a black Kenyan father, Barack Obama Sr. The couple met while they were students at the University of Hawaii. They soon married and had a son. But the marriage did not last. A year after they married, Obama Sr. left his wife and son in Hawaii to study at Harvard University. After living apart for most of their marriage, the couple divorced in 1964, and Obama Sr. returned to Kenya, abandoning his American son.

A year later Ann married an Indonesian man, and in 1967 she moved with her son to Indonesia. Life there was not easy for the boy. He was stared at and teased because of his multiethnic appearance. Outwardly, Barack did not react to this mistreatment. Knowing that mixed-race people often faced racial slurs and discrimination, his mother raised him to be self-controlled, calm, and seemingly fearless—character traits that she thought would help him cope with the challenges he might face.

When Barack was nine years old, his mother gave birth to his half-sister, Maya. A year later, Ann sent Barack back to Hawaii to live with his maternal grandparents and go to school there.

Life in the United States

Barack got a scholarship to Punahou Academy, a prestigious private school that he attended for eight years. It was during his adolescence that he began wrestling with his ethnic identity. As one of only three students of African descent, he was unsure where he fit in, both in school and in society. He was a multiracial boy with African features, abandoned by his black father, and raised by a white mother and white grandparents. Because of his appearance, most people classified him as African American. As he matured, he came to accept this identity. "I realized that if the world saw me as African-American that was not something I needed to run away from, that was something I needed to embrace," he explains. "I am less interested in how we label ourselves. I am more interested in how we treat each other. And if we are treating each other right, I can be African-American; I can be multiracial; I can be you name it. What matters is, am I showing people respect, am I caring for other people?"[40]

> "I am less interested in how we label ourselves. I am more interested in how we treat each other."[40]
>
> —Barack Obama, the forty-fourth president of the United States

After graduating from Punahou, Obama attended Columbia University, where he earned a degree in political science in 1983. He then worked as a community organizer in an impoverished area of Chicago. During this time he went to Kenya, where he met his African relatives and visited the graves of his father and grandfather. This trip helped him connect the different aspects of his life and heritage. He recalls, "For a long time I sat between the two graves and wept. I saw that my life in America—the black life, the white life. . .—all of it was connected with this small plot of earth an ocean away."[41]

Returning from Africa with a new sense of self, and a growing desire to help the less fortunate, Obama enrolled in Harvard Law School, where he was a star student. According to Professor Laurence Tribe, "The better he did at Harvard Law School and the more he impressed people, the more obvious it became that he could have had anything, but it was clear that he wanted to make a difference to people, to communities."[42]

Obama has made a difference. In 2008 he became the first multiracial president of the United States and won reelection in 2012. During his time in office, he created and supported laws and policies that fostered tolerance and worked hard toward the goal of equal treatment of all Americans no matter their race, religion, gender, or sexual orientation. He also advocated for human rights throughout the world. For his efforts in promoting cooperation between people and nations, he was awarded the Nobel Peace Prize in 2009.

Obama's legacy has inspired many multiethnic young people. Grace Gibson, a mixed-race teen, says his legacy "embodies change and hope for so many in this country of all generations, genders, races and cultures. His message of bringing us all together as Americans is enhanced by his mixed heritage. . . . So one should feel nothing but pride to be mixed in America."[43]

Special, Not Different

Meghan Markle, the American actress, activist, and recent bride of Great Britain's Prince Harry, is also multiracial. She is the daughter of Doria Raglandan, a black clinical therapist, and Thomas Markle, a white television lighting director. Meghan was born on August 4, 1981, in Los Angeles and grew up there. Her parents raised her to feel that she and her family were special, but not different or abnormal. To reinforce the family's normalcy, one Christmas Meghan's parents gave her a family of dolls that consisted of a black mother doll, a white father doll, and two children, one of each color. She recalls,

> When I was about seven, I had been fawning over a boxed set of Barbie dolls. It was called The Heart Family and included a mom doll, a dad doll, and two children. This perfect nuclear family was only sold in sets of white dolls or black dolls. I don't remember coveting one over the other, I just wanted one. On Christmas morning, swathed in glitter-flecked wrapping paper, there I found my Heart Family: a black mom doll, a white dad doll, and a child in each color. My dad had taken the sets apart and customized my family.[44]

Multiracial Celebrities

As the multiracial population continues to increase, there are more and more multiracial individuals helping to shape society. Many of these people work in the entertainment industry. These include musical artists such as Zendaya, Mariah Carey, Shakira, and Alicia Keys, among many others. Many actors are also multiracial. Dwayne Johnson, Rashida Jones, Shemar Moore, Hailee Steinfeld, Cameron Diaz, and Yara Shahidi are just a few of many mixed-race actors. Others include Halle Berry, Keanu Reeves, Tracee Ellis Ross, Maya Rudolph, and Olivia Munn.

Other multiracial individuals are champions in sports. Individuals such as former captain of the New York Yankees Derek Jeter, golf great Tiger Woods, tennis star Madison Keys, and Olympic swimming gold medalist Ryan Lochte are all mixed race. So is quarterback and political activist Colin Kaepernick. Other mixed-race people, such as US senators Corey Booker, Kamala Harris, and Tammy Duckworth, are making their mark in government. Still other mixed-race individuals are successful writers, journalists, artists, businesspeople, and scientists. Indeed, multiracial people are changing the face of the United States.

Growing up, Meghan embraced her multiracial heritage—and her family. She says, "I have the most vivid memories of being seven years old and my mom picking me up from my grandmother's house. There were the three of us, a family tree in an ombré [shades of a color] of mocha next to the caramel complexion of my mom and light-skinned, freckled me. I remember the sense of belonging, having nothing to do with the color of my skin."[45]

Meghan felt so secure in her multiracial identity that in seventh grade, when she was instructed to complete a section of a survey indicating her ethnicity, she refused to do so because there was no place to designate hers as multiracial. The choices were black, white, Hispanic, or Asian. "You could only choose one, but that

Meghan Markle, now England's Duchess of Sussex, is the daughter of a mixed-race marriage. Although she was aware of racial differences when she was a child, her loving family raised her to believe her multiracial identity was special, not abnormal.

would be to choose one parent over the other—and one half of myself over the other," she explains. "My teacher told me to check the box for Caucasian. 'Because that's how you look, Meghan,' she said. I put down my pen. Not as an act of defiance, but rather a symptom of my confusion. I couldn't bring myself to do that, to picture the pit-in-her-belly sadness my mother would feel if she were to find out. So, I didn't tick [check] a box. I left my identity blank."[46]

Although she was never defiant, young Meghan was not afraid of speaking out. She was raised to be compassionate toward the disenfranchised and to stand up for what she thought was right. So, at age eleven, she waged a letter-writing campaign against a dishwashing soap commercial that she felt promoted an unfair stereotype of women. As a result of her efforts alone, the manufacturer changed the commercial. "It was at that moment that I realized the magnitude of my actions,"[47] she explains. Since that time she has continued to speak up for, and take actions that support, what she thinks is right.

> "I wasn't black enough for the black roles and I wasn't white enough for the white ones, leaving me somewhere in the middle as the ethnic chameleon who couldn't book a job."[48]
>
> —Actress and activist Meghan Markle

An Influential Woman

After finishing high school, Markle went on to graduate from Northwestern University with a double major in theater and international studies. She was determined to become an actress but found that her ambiguous appearance and multiethnic background often stood in her way. She explains, "I wasn't black enough for the black roles and I wasn't white enough for the white ones, leaving me somewhere in the middle as the ethnic chameleon who couldn't book a job."[48]

Eventually Markle began landing small roles. Her big break came in 2011, when she was cast as Rachel Zane in the television series *Suits*. "The show's producers weren't looking for someone mixed, nor someone white or black for that matter. They were simply looking for Rachel,"[49] she says.

The role made Markle a celebrity. In the ensuing years she used her fame as a platform to champion a variety of philanthropic projects. Her activism and support for charitable causes is one of many interests she shares with Prince Harry. The two met on a blind date in 2016 and have been in a relationship ever since then.

Because of the tremendous media interest in the prince's private life, the couple tried to keep their relationship under wraps in order to protect their privacy. Once it became public, Markle was subjected to a number of defamatory articles and racist comments on social media and in British tabloids. Prince Harry criticized those articles and comments, and the two announced their engagement in 2017.

As the first mixed-race member of the British royal family, Markle is a symbol of the changing face of British families. According to the British Office for National Statistics, one in ten people in Great Britain are in a mixed-race relationship. Markle and the prince have received a lot of support from these individuals. Shantania Beckford, a woman of Jamaican descent, is part of this group. "People will be a lot more accepting of mixed couples now, and talk about interracial issues,"[50] she says.

The match is also supported by Prince Harry's family, but there are still people who question whether a mixed-race person should be part of the royal family. Markle disagrees. She says that she is proud "to say who I am, to share where I'm from, to voice my pride in being a strong, confident mixed-race woman."[51]

Surrounded by Music

Grammy Award–winner Bruno Mars is another celebrity who is proud of his mixed heritage. Born Peter Gene Hernandez on October 8, 1985, in Hawaii, he was nicknamed "Bruno" when he was a toddler, and the name stuck. According to his older sister, Jamie, "Bruno was always so confident, independent, really strong-willed, and kind of a brute—hence the name Bruno."[52]

Bruno grew up as one of six children in a multiethnic musical family. From the cradle on, he was surrounded by music. His fa-

Celebrating Multiracial America

Since 2013, a festival that celebrates multiracial people has been an annual event. The festival, known as the Mixed Remixed Festival, is held at the Japanese American National Museum in Los Angeles. It is the largest meeting of multiracial people and families in the nation. According to the festival's website, "The Mixed Remixed Festival brings together film and book lovers, innovative and emerging artists, and multiracial families and individuals, Hapas, and families of transracial adoption."

Festivalgoers take part in a range of activities that celebrate multiracialism. They listen to storytellers, attend movie screenings and author readings, and see live performances by mixed race actors, musicians, and comedians. A variety of workshops and panel discussions are held on issues related to the unique experiences that multiethnic people have. There are special activities geared toward children and families that include interactive arts and crafts and storytelling, sing-alongs, face painting, and collaborative family projects. In addition, the festival provides attendees the opportunity to meet and connect with other multiracial individuals and families, which is important since many mixed-race people feel isolated.

Mixed Remixed, "About." www.mixedremixed.org.

ther, Pete, is a percussionist of Puerto Rican and Jewish heritage, and his mother, Bernadette, was a Filipino singer and hula dancer. When Bruno was a boy, Pete led a family band that included Bruno's mother, uncles, and older siblings. The group performed all kinds of music and did celebrity impersonations. Almost as soon as he could walk, Bruno started singing and playing music. "Everyone in my family sings, plays instruments. It's what we do," he says. "I've always had a drum set, a piano, a guitar . . . and never got trained to play. It was just always there. That's just how I learned, just being surrounded by it my whole life."[53]

In addition to making music, at three years old Bruno began doing Elvis Presley impersonations. He spent hours watching videotapes of Presley while wiggling his hips and crooning into an

Pop music icon Bruno Mars has parents that possess Puerto Rican, Jewish, and Filipino heritages. Refusing to be stereotyped as a Latin artist, Mars has developed a mix of musical styles that appeals to a wide range of listeners.

imaginary microphone. By the time he was four, he was performing his impersonation on stage with the band. People flocked to see him. His father recalls, "He was the star of the show and I had him on a platform because you could barely see him on the stage he was so tiny."[54]

Superstar

Bruno's parents divorced when he was around twelve years old, and the family band broke up. In 2003, after graduating from high school, he moved to Los Angeles with dreams of becoming a superstar. When he tried to break into the music industry, his ethnicity became an issue. Industry executives wanted Bruno to describe himself as Puerto Rican and to focus on writing and performing Latin music. Yet Bruno did not want to reject his multiracial identity or create music geared to just one ethnic group. He believes that music transcends race: "How are you going to tell me that this song that I'm writing is only going to be catered to Puerto Ricans or to white people or only Asian people? How are you going to tell me that? My music is for anybody who wants to listen to it."[55]

To avoid being stereotyped by race, he began using the stage name Bruno Mars. Yet because he resisted changing the way he identified himself and refused to perform only one particular musical genre, Mars found it difficult to break into the music industry as a performer. As a result, he started writing and producing songs for other artists. After those songs became big hits, he was featured as a guest singer on other artists' albums. By 2010 he had become a solo artist. The genuine pleasure he took in performing, the happy sound of his music, his slick dance moves, and his trademark fedora hat, endeared him to the public and made him a superstar.

> "You have to be who you are and hopefully they dig it."[56]
> —Bruno Mars, musical artist

Since then, he has won numerous accolades, including nine Grammy Awards. He was the headline performer of the 2013 Super Bowl halftime show and a featured guest performer in 2015. Today Mars's music is played all over the world. Just as his heritage is a mix of ethnicities, so, too, is his music a mix of genres. Despite being told he would fail, he remained true to himself, his multiracial identity, and his dream of making music that crossed racial boundaries. In so doing, he has made it easier for other multiethnic artists to follow their dreams. "You have to be who you are," he insists, "and hopefully they dig it."[56]

Chapter Five

Exploring Identity

Growing up in a multiracial family has advantages and disadvantages. These young people cope with many of the same issues as kids who are raised in other kinds of families, but they also struggle with establishing their cultural identity. Unlike single race individuals whose cultural identity is clear, multiracial kids and teens cannot easily define who they are. Jason Klanderud, a multiethnic blogger, recalls standing in front of a mirror and pondering the meaning of his ethnicity: "I started doing that years ago. . . . Standing there I'd ask the questions to myself. 'What am I looking at?'. . . You see, everyone else in my life that was more or less considered one 'race' didn't seem to have to answer this question for themselves. But I had to."[57]

Some young people come to identify with one culture, but others embrace multiple cultures. For many, the way they identify is fluid. They may identify with one part of their background as adolescents, for example. Then, as they mature and discover more about themselves and their place in society, the way they identify may change. As one young man explains, "There was a time when I didn't identify as black. In fact, growing up I really hung onto this idea that I was biracial. . . . It wasn't 'til college that I made that switch from identifying as biracial to being black."[58]

Yet no matter the cultural identity that they settle upon, over time most multiethnic young people come to realize that they are special and play an important role in society. Grace Gibson, a mixed-race teenager, points out that

> the biracial [or multiracial] person personifies the breaking down of racial barriers that so many fought and died for in the civil rights movement. It is what Dr. Martin Luther King

stood for and what his legacy of equality imparts to us to-day. . . . I am proud to be a child born to two loving, talent-ed, creative people—a mother and father who happened to be of African-American and English descent, respectively. . . . I am the melting pot, and in our global society, soon all the children of the world will be a mixture of races as well.[59]

Exploring My Roots

Growing up, most kids face identity issues. Young people question who they are and what their place is in society, among other things. For multiracial kids and teens, part of answering these questions usually involves establishing their ethnic identity. Doing so often in-volves exploring the different aspects of their cultural heritage.

For a number of reasons, some kids do not know a lot about all of their background. Many young people are raised in families in which only one part of their cultural heritage is emphasized. This often occurs when children are raised by a single parent who is not knowledgeable about the absent parent's culture and therefore deemphasizes it. This was the case for Meghan Dooley, a young woman whose mother is of Irish and German descent and whose father is African American. She explains, "My parents weren't together during the time I was being raised. In fact, I've never had any sort of relationship with my father at all. That ob-stacle alone made it difficult for me to fully understand my biracial identity. . . . I don't really have any cultural connection or traditions in . . . that aspect of my life!"[60]

But even when young people are exposed to multiple cultures, some still feel less connected to some aspects of their heritage than they do to other aspects. Language barriers or geographic distances that prevent them from communicating with or getting to know extended family members often lead to this feeling. The racial makeup of the neighborhood in which young people grow up, the schools they attend, and the ethnicity of their friends also impact what cultures they are exposed to and whether or not they feel linked to all of their cultural heritage. Meilina Wilkinson, a young woman of Taiwanese and English heritage, recalls, "I grew up in Long Island [New York]. It was a pretty white suburban type of experience. . . . I identified as more white than Asian because that was my experience—that was who my friends were, that was what they considered me."[61]

Teens and young adults, in particular, do many things in an effort to explore their roots. Among other activities, they enroll in classes, join clubs, do extensive reading, or learn a language if one is associated with the culture they are exploring. For instance, to learn more about her Asian side, Wilkinson joined an Asian American club in college and started learning Mandarin. "It's your choice whether to identify with one particular group," she says, "but I think it's important to acknowledge all of yourself."[62]

Many young people visit the country of their forebears in order to directly experience that part of their culture as well as to meet and connect with distant relatives. The experience can help individuals feel closer to that part of their background. For example, Gino Pellegrini, a man whose mother is Hispanic and father is Italian, had limited contact with his father while growing up. After graduating from high school, Pellegrini went to Italy to track down his father and meet his Italian relatives. The experience helped him appreciate and become more comfortable with the Italian side of his heritage. He says, "The time I spent with my family and my father in Italy showed me that it was possible to develop an international, multiethnic sense of self."[63]

> "The time I spent with my family and my father in Italy showed me that it was possible to develop an international, multiethnic sense of self."[63]
>
> —Gino Pellegrini, a multiethnic man

In other instances, such a journey can make individuals feel even less connected to that part of their cultural roots. Sometimes that happens when expectations are too high. Those who imagine they will be enamored with the culture, embraced by the native population, and fit in better there than they do back home sometimes experience disappointment.

Many young people with multiracial backgrounds explore their heritages by traveling to the lands of their forebears. This experience allows them to connect with distant family and gain a better understanding of the history and lifestyle of those cultures.

In some situations, these young people's ambiguous appearances label them as outsiders. In others, they find that the values they grew up with and adhere to conflict with those of the local culture. When Brian, a young man whose mother is Japanese American and whose father is white, went to Japan to explore his cultural heritage, he found that his appearance marked him as an outsider. As a result, although he was treated courteously, he never felt like he fit in. "It made me realize, 'If I'm in Japan, no one is going to accept me as Japanese.' It made me think, 'Okay, check that off my list—I'm definitely not Japanese.' That was maybe a little disappointing. But it wasn't such a negative thing for me, it was more of a revelatory experience,"[64] he explains.

Identifying with One Culture

After exploring their ethnic roots, some young people come to embrace one particular part of their ethnic background over another. Often, they make this choice because of the way they are

Identifying as Native American

Mixed-race young people of Native American descent who choose to become a member of a particular tribe face hurdles that other multiethnic individuals do not. In the United States, laws known as blood quantum laws, are often used to define who can be a member of a Native American tribe. These laws are based on a person's degree of Native American ancestry. For example, a person with one single-race Native American parent and one non–Native American parent has a blood quantum of one half. If that individual has a child with a non–Native American partner, the child would have a blood quantum of one-quarter, and so on.

Under the Indian Reorganization Act of 1934, the federal government required individuals to have a certain blood quantum to be recognized as Native American and be eligible for financial benefits under federal treaties. During the twenty-first century, although anyone can identify as Native American, each tribe sets its own rules that define who can become a tribal member. Rules vary, but many tribes still use blood quantum requirements to define membership. Requirements range from one-half to one-thirty-second blood quantum, depending on the tribe. Strict blood quantum requirements can make it difficult for some mixed-race young people to be accepted as a tribal member in certain tribes. Other tribes have less demanding laws that allow some multiracial individuals to become tribal members and become more deeply involved in that part of their background.

treated by others and the way society views them. This is particularly true for people who are part black. Historically, in the United States a person with any traceable sub-Saharan African lineage was considered to be black. This was known as the one-drop law. It was enacted to keep multiracial individuals from identifying or passing as white, thereby obtaining the higher social status that being white afforded people. Although the one-drop law is no longer in effect and racial discrimination is prohibited, some prejudiced Americans still accept the concept of the one-drop law. These people view mixed race individuals of African American descent as black, and they often treat them unfairly. According to American statesman and retired five-star general Colin Powell, who comes from a multigenerational mixed-race background, "In America, which I love from the depths of my heart and soul, when you look like me, you're black."[65]

Similarly, other mixed-race people are often discriminated against and classified by others based on their minority heritage. According to Diana Sanchez, an associate professor of psychology at Rutgers University and an expert on multiracial experiences, "A lot of research points [out that] mixed-race people tend to be perceived along the lines of their minority identity."[66]

Therefore, based on the way they are treated and viewed by society, many multiethnic people tend to identify solely with their minority background. Many of these young people also feel that identifying as single race is a way to show support for racial minorities as well as to protest and resist racism. As Matthew Braunginn, a mixed-race civil rights activist who identifies as black, explains,

> "A lot of research points [out that] mixed-race people tend to be perceived along the lines of their minority identity."[66]
>
> —Diana Sanchez, an associate professor of psychology at Rutgers University

I can be in a group of white people that is in the middle of an encounter with cops, and the officers somehow are more aggressive towards me than the white people around me. I learned, through being aware enough of my experiences, that I am not white, nor will I ever be. . . . So I claim my black identity with pride, as I want nothing to do with the legacy of white supremacy and want to help this nation break free of that.[67]

Embracing a single-race identity is not limited to individuals who are discriminated against or are protesting racial inequality. Some multiethnic individuals choose to classify themselves as a single race because they feel closest to one particular element of their heritage. Tyonek, for example, is a young man of Mexican, European, and Native American descent. He grew up on the Quinault Reservation observing Native American customs, ceremonies, and traditions. Although he is knowledgeable about the different parts of his background, he identifies as Native American because he adheres to those cultural values. He says that this culture is closest to his heart.

Many Parts Form a Whole

Although many kids and teens are comfortable identifying with a single culture, others are not. Many of these young people insist that the different parts of their heritage cannot be separated or divided; rather, they believe they blend together like ingredients in a recipe to form a whole. These individuals embrace each part of their cultural heritage and define themselves as multiracial, multiethnic, mixed race, or biracial, among other similar terms. They make this choice for a variety of reasons. Some feel that if they identify as single race, they are choosing one parent over another or, worse, rejecting one of their parents and that parent's impact on their life. This is how Megan McDonald, a mixed-race young woman who identifies as multiracial, feels. As she explains,

> "I can't simply leave one [culture] to adopt the other. My dad had an impact on my life, as did my mom. . . . I refuse to subscribe to just one race."[68]
>
> —Megan McDonald, a mixed-race young woman

I can't simply leave one [culture] to adopt the other. My dad had an impact on my life, as did my mom. Would I be doing an injustice to my upbringing by rejecting my white identity, or even worse, seem as if I didn't value my dad? And as for my mom, with all her love and tenderness, would I inadvertently reject her and her culture by abandoning my Filipino background? I refuse to subscribe to just one race.[68]

Most mixed-race young people are proud of the cultures they represent. Some feel their unique identities can help bring different communities together; others happily anticipate that their uniqueness will fade as society gets used to more and more multiracial families.

In addition to feeling that identifying with only one culture is a rejection of part of their family, some young people believe that it is also a rejection of part of themselves. "We all hold multiple identities that make up who we are at any given time," says Michael Chrzan, a young man who identifies as biracial. "It is not any of those singular identities that define us, but how they come together in each of us, uniquely."[69]

I Am Unique and Special

No matter what culture or cultures multiracial kids and teens choose to identify with, as they look at themselves and explore their roots, most come to appreciate who they are and the special role that they and their families play in society. Indeed, many people view mixed-race young people as agents of change. They believe that as the multiracial population continues to grow, intermarry, and reproduce, it will become increasingly difficult to distinguish between racial groups. Therefore, racial stereotyping will be hard to do, and racism will become a thing of the past.

Studying Multiracial Identity

Currently there is not a lot of research related to multiracial people. Sarah Gaither is trying to change that. Gaither is an assistant professor of psychology and neuroscience at Duke University. She is also the head researcher in Duke's Identity and Diversity Lab, a research facility dedicated to studying issues related to race, identity, and cultural diversity. Gaither, whose mother is white and father is black, identifies as multiracial. Growing up multiracial sparked her interest in studying multiracial people.

One area Gaither is researching is how multiracial people often take on different cultural identities at different times in their lives, and how this behavior affects multiracial people and society. According to Gaither,

> What a lot of our work is trying to argue is that if you are biracial or have these multiple identities, this actually leads to what we call "identity flexibility." You're able to cross diverse spaces more easily compared to people from monoracial backgrounds. . . . It really highlights this malleability of biracial individuals and the fact that they might have an extra tool to help navigate different types of spaces.

If Gaither's theory proves to be correct, mixed-race people may very well be uniquely qualified to serve as a bridge between different cultural groups—just as some multiracial young people suggest.

Quoted in Karson Baldwin, "Famous Friday: Dr Sarah Gaither," Project Race, February 22, 2018. www.projectrace.com.

This theory assumes that such blending will eliminate visual traits that serve as racial identifiers, like skin color. However, genetics are complex. There is no way to predict how a mixed-race person will look. Likewise, the possibility that racial identifiers will disappear is questionable. However, many multiracial individuals do feel that, no matter how they look, they can help make the world a better place. They believe that their experiences make them open to different cultures and tolerant of people of different backgrounds. As Ki Mae, a multiethnic young woman, asserts, "The more of a mix a person becomes—of experiences, of ethnicities, of cultures that are racial or not—the more she becomes connected to other people, the more she is able to understand and the more she is [able] to share."[70]

Some multiracial individuals believe that because they can move between different cultures, they can act as a bridge or a voice between diverse ethnic groups. "My identity makes me stand out," says Yuki, a mixed-race young woman. "I spent high school being acutely aware of being a minority but not knowing what to do about it. I spent college being proud of being a student of color and organizing communities around the shared experience. . . . I know that my experiences and knowledge matter, I'm happy that my background and experiences gave me access to many spaces and groups."[71]

Indeed, although multiracial young people face unique challenges growing up and often struggle with their identity, most are proud of who they are and the distinctive perspective they have. A 2015 Pew Research Center survey of 1,555 multiracial Americans found that 60 percent of those surveyed are proud of their mixed background. As Shava, a multiethnic young woman, expresses, "At times it can be confusing. I have wondered where I fit in. But in the end . . . I'm so glad to have the depth of experience that being multicultural has given me. I'm black, white and I'm Jewish. It's amazing!"[72]

Source Notes

Chapter One: How American Families Are Changing

1. Quoted in Pearl Fuyo Gaskins, *What Are You?* New York: Holt, 1999, p. 37.
2. Quoted in Susan Saulny, "Census Data Presents Rise in Multiracial Population of Youths," *New York Times*, March 24, 2011. www.nytimes.com.
3. E. Dolores Johnson, "The Census Always Boxed Us Out," *Narratively*, October 30, 2017. http://narrative.ly.
4. George Yancey and Richard Lewis Jr., *Interracial Families*. New York: Routledge, 2009, p. 5.
5. Quoted in Pew Research Center, "Chapter 5: Race and Social Connections—Friends, Family and Neighborhoods," *Multiracial in America*, June 11, 2015. www.pewsocialtrends.org.
6. Kathleen Ojo, "Ruminations on Race," *Mixed Space* (blog), October 8, 2014. www.mixedspace.org.
7. Quoted in Tanya Hutchins, *Born Beautiful Biracial*. Alexandria, VA: TP Rewards, 2014, p. 10.
8. Quoted in Raising Mothers, "Meet Rachelle Chapman." www.raisingmothers.com.

Chapter Two: How I See Myself and My Family

9. Allison Bates, "A Sort of Hybrid," in *Mixed*, ed. Andrew Garrod, Robert Kilkenny, and Christina Gomez. Ithaca, NY: Cornell University Press, 2014, p. 53.
10. Quoted in Gaskins, *What Are You?*, p. 173.
11. Quoted in *Talk of the Nation*, "Multiracial Identity in America Today," NPR, April 6, 2007. www.npr.org.
12. Quoted in Hutchins, *Born Beautiful Biracial*, p. 22.
13. Nadra Kareem Nittle, "Raising Biracial Children to Be Well Adjusted," ThoughtCo., March 18, 2017. www.thoughtco.com.
14. Chris Collado, "So, What Are You?," in *Mixed*, ed. Garrod, Kilkenny, and Gomez, p. 32.
15. Fariba Soetan, "Seven Reasons Why I Love My Mixed Race Family," *Huffington Post*, October 4, 2016. www.huffingtonpost.co.uk.
16. Quoted in Gaskins, *What Are You?*, p. 177.

17. Quoted in Frances Kai-Hwa Wang, "Diving into Race, Identity of Multiracial Families in 'Raising Mixed Race,'" NBC News, December 31, 2015. www.nbcnews.com.
18. Jennifer Noble, "Meeting My Mix," *Mixed Space* (blog), August 26, 2014. www.mixedspace.org.
19. Quoted in Andrew Garrod, Robert Kilkenny, and Christina Gomez, eds., introduction to *Mixed*, p. 10.
20. Garrod, Kilkenny, and Gomez, eds., introduction to *Mixed*, p. 10.
21. Quoted in Corinne Segal, "How Poet Ariana Brown Became the Afro-Latina Role Model She Needed," *PBS NewsHour*, February 8, 2016. www.pbs.org.
22. Quoted in Bossip Staff, "Rashida Jones' Sister Kidada Agrees 'She Passed for White' but Did the Mean Girls at Harvard Scare Her Away from Dating Black Men Forever?," Bossip, August 6, 2012. https://bossip.com.
23. Quoted in Bossip Staff, "Rashida Jones' Sister Kidada Agrees 'She Passed for White' but Did the Mean Girls at Harvard Scare Her Away from Dating Black Men Forever?"
24. Quoted in Bustle, "18 Mixed Raced Celebrities Who Are Diversifying Hollywood." www.bustle.com.

Chapter Three: How Others See Me and My Family

25. Quoted in Gaskins, *What Are You?*, p. 74.
26. Quoted in *Talk of the Nation*, "Multiracial Identity in America Today."
27. Quoted in Hutchins, *Born Beautiful Biracial*, p. 40.
28. Ealoni Friedenthal, "Memoirs of an Uncharacteristic Biracial Child: The World Is Not So Black and White," *Mixed Space* (blog), August 26, 2014. www.mixedspace.org.
29. Nevin Martell, "That Awful Moment Parents of Interracial Children Will Probably Face," *Washington Post*, April 26, 2016. www.washingtonpost.com.
30. Nicole S. Chung, "'Mixed Kids Are Always So Beautiful,'" *Motherlode* (blog), *New York Times*, August 19, 2013. https://parenting.blogs.nytimes.com.
31. *Alanna & Company* (blog), "On Being Multiracial," February 2016. www.alannaandcompany.com.
32. Jordan Gee, "½ Black; ¼ Chinese; ¼ Norwegian," Race Card Project, January 22, 2018. http://theracecardproject.com.
33. Amber, "Being 'Mixed' Race Is Super Frustrating," Race Card Project. https://theracecardproject.com.
34. Quoted in Garrod, Kilkenny, and Gomez, eds., introduction to *Mixed*, p. 7.

35. Quoted in Joyce A. Ladner, *Mixed Families*. New York: Anchor, 1977, p. 25.
36. Quoted in ClydeLovesMariah, "Mariah Carey Talking About Her Struggles of Being Bi-racial on Oprah Winfrey in 1999," YouTube, April 10, 2012. www.youtube.com.
37. Quoted in Gaskins, *What Are You?*, p. 90.
38. Quoted in Gaskins, *What Are You?*, pp. 221–22.
39. Quoted in Hutchins, *Born Beautiful Biracial*, p. 45.

Chapter Four: Other People Who Have Families Like Mine

40. Quoted in MultiracialHeritage, "Barack Obama on Being Bi-racial on 'The View,'" YouTube, March 24, 2011. www.youtube.com.
41. Quoted in Biography.com, "Barack Obama." www.biography.com.
42. Quoted in Biography.com, "Barack Obama."
43. Lynn Whitfield and Grace Gibson, "I'm Neither Black nor White—I'm Both (Blog), CNN's Black in America," Mixed Heritage Center. www.mixedheritagecenter.org.
44. Quoted in Angelina Pronto, "Biracial Actress Meghan Markle Opens Up About Her Ethnicity: 7 Lessons You Can Learn," *Entity*, April 3, 2017. www.entitymag.com.
45. Quoted in Brittany Stephens, "What Bothers Meghan Markle Most About Being Biracial in Hollywood," Pop Sugar, March 25, 2017. www.popsugar.com.
46. Quoted in Ainhoa Barcelona, "Meghan Markle Pens Powerful Post About Being Biracial," *Hello!*, March 28, 2016. http://us.hellomagazine.com.
47. Quoted in Lisa Respers France and Judith Vonberg, "Meghan Markle Is Royal Family's Unconventional Bride-to-Be," CNN, November 28, 2017. www.cnn.com.
48. Quoted in France and Vonberg, "Meghan Markle Is Royal Family's Unconventional Bride-to-Be."
49. Quoted in Barcelona, "Meghan Markle Pens Powerful Post About Being Biracial."
50. Quoted in Joice Etutu, "Harry and Meghan: Inter-racial Couples React to the Royal Engagement," BBC News, November 27, 2017. www.bbc.com.
51. Quoted in Barcelona, "Meghan Markle Pens Powerful Post About Being Biracial."
52. Quoted in Biography.com, "Bruno Mars." www.biography.com.

53. Quoted in Biography.com, "Bruno Mars."
54. Quoted in Hawaii News Now, "One-on-One with Bruno Mars' Dad on His Superstar Son," 2014. www.hawaiinewsnow.com.
55. Quoted in Rap-Up, "Bruno Mars Opens Up About Race, Discrimination & Loss of His Mother," January 30, 2017. www.rap-up.com.
56. Quoted in AZquotes, "Bruno Mars Quotes." www.azquotes.com.

Chapter Five: Exploring Identity

57. Jason Klanderud, "Coping Introspection," *Mix Communities* (blog), July 26, 2008. http://mixcommunities.blogspot.com.
58. Quoted in Pew Research Center, "Chapter 3: The Multiracial Identity Gap," *Multiracial in America*, July 11, 2015. www.pewsocialtrends.org.
59. Whitfield and Gibson, "I'm Neither Black nor White."
60. Quoted in Jen Fisch, "Featured Multiracial Individual: Meet Meghan Dooley," Multiracial Media, November 11, 2016. http://multiracialmedia.com.
61. Quoted in Gaskins, *What Are You?*, p. 190.
62. Quoted in Gaskins, *What Are You?*, p. 191.
63. Gino Pellegrini, "On Growing Up Mexican Italian American," *Parent Voice*, January 8, 2018. www.theparentvoice.com.
64. Quoted in Gaskins, *What Are You?*, p. 175.
65. Quoted in Nadra Kareem Nittle, "Five Myths About Multiracial People in the U.S.," ThoughtCo., March 18, 2017. www.thoughtco.com.
66. Quoted in Alexandros Orphanides, "Why Mixed-Race Americans Will Not Save the Country," *Code Switching* (blog), NPR, March 8, 2017. www.npr.org.
67. Quoted in Henry Sanders, "Best of 2016: 12 on Tuesday with Matthew Braunginn," Madison 365. http://madison365.com.
68. Megan McDonald, "Viewpoint: Living in Racial Limbo," *Michigan Daily*, November 12, 2013. www.michigandaily.com.
69. Michael Chrzan, "Michigan in Color: Authenticity," *Michigan Daily*, January 20, 2016. www.michigandaily.com.
70. Ki Mae Ponniah Heussner, "A Little Plot of No-Man's Land," in *Mixed*, ed. Garrod, Kilkenny, and Gomez, p. 108.
71. Yuki Kondo-Shah, "In My World 1 + 1 = 3," in *Mixed*, ed. Garrod, Kilkenny, and Gomez, p. 52.
72. Shava, "Mixed and I Love My Perspective," Race Card Project. https://theracecardproject.com.

Books

Noah Berlatsky, *Multiracial America*. Farmington Hills, MI: Greenhaven, 2013.

Sharon H. Chang, *Raising Mixed Race: Multiracial Asian Children in a Post-racial World*. New York: Routledge, 2016.

Hal Marcovitz, *Teens and Race*. Broomall, PA: Mason Crest, 2014.

H.W. Poole, *Multiracial Families*. Broomall, PA: Mason Crest, 2017.

Joanne L. Rondilla, Rudy P. Guevarra Jr., and Paul Spickard, eds., *Red and Yellow, Black and Brown: Decentering Whiteness in Mixed Race Studies*. New Brunswick, NJ: Rutgers University Press, 2017.

Internet Sources

Lexi Brock, as told to Kim Tranell, "What Are You?," Scholastic, April 2017. https://choices.scholastic.com/issues/2016-17/040 117/what-are-you.html.

Audrey Carlson, "See Me as I Am: Kids Tell Us What It Is Like to Be Multiracial in Seattle," *Seattle Times*, August 18, 2016. www .seattletimes.com/pacific-nw-magazine/see-me-as-i-am-kids -tell-us-what-its-like-to-be-multiracial-in-seattle.

Pew Research Center, *Multiracial in America*, July 11, 2015. www .pewsocialtrends.org/2015/06/11/multiracial-in-america.

Organizations and Websites

Loving Day (www.lovingday.org). Loving Day is an organization that fights racism and promotes multicultural diversity. It offers information about *Loving v. Virginia* and sponsors annual Loving Day events that celebrate multiracial families.

Mixed Heritage Center (www.mixedheritagecenter.org). The Mixed Heritage Center provides information and resources related to the lives of multiracial people.

Mixed Space (www.mixedspace.org). *Mixed Space* is a blog that provides articles and personal accounts about transracial adoptions and what it is like being mixed race.

Project Race (www.projectrace.com). Project Race is an organization that advocates for multiracial people and their families through education. It provides information about issues concerning multiracial people, including special sections for children and teens and interviews with multiracial individuals.

Race Card Project (https://theracecardproject.com). The Race Card Project is a project in which people from all over submit short essays about race and culture. Many of the submissions deal with issues related to being multiracial.

US Census Bureau (www.census.gov). The US Census Bureau gathers data about life in the United States. Its website has a variety of information related to multiracial people and families.

Index